The Viking Explorers

Explorers of New Worlds

Explorers of New Worlds

The Viking Explorers

Jim Gallagher

Chelsea House Publishers
Philadelphia

For the Vikings of C-14:
Larry T., Rick S., Mike J., and Kevin K.

Prepared for Chelsea House Publishers by:
OTTN Publishing, Stockton, N.J.

CHELSEA HOUSE PUBLISHERS
Production Manager: Pamela Loos
Art Director: Sara Davis
Director of Photography: Judy L. Hasday
Managing Editor: James D. Gallagher
Senior Production Editor: J. Christopher Higgins
Series Designer: Keith Trego
Cover Design: Forman Group

First Printing
1 3 5 7 9 8 6 4 2

Library of Congress Cataloging-in-Publication Data

Gallagher, Jim, 1969-
    The Viking explorers / Jim Gallagher.
        p.   cm. – (Explorers of new worlds)
Includes bibliographical references and index.
ISBN 0-7910-5955-3 (hc) – ISBN 0-7910-6165-5 (pbk.)
1. Vikings–Juvenile literature. 2. Discoveries in geography–Scandinavian–Juvenile literature. 3. Explorers–
Scandinavia–Juvenile literature. [1. Vikings. 2. Explorers.] I. Title. II. Series.

DL65 G35 2000
910'.948'0902–dc21

                                        00-034598

Contents

The Unknown Lands to the West

A replica of a Viking ship cruises through the Atlantic Ocean at sunset. The Vikings were the greatest sailors and adventurers of the Middle Ages. While the other peoples of Europe were content to stay close to the coasts, the Vikings ranged far into the Atlantic.

I

The rough, bearded men clutched at the sides of their long, wooden ship as foaming waves crashed and icy winds blew around them. The year was A.D. 986, and these brave sailors were caught in a fierce storm in the North Atlantic Ocean. For three days, the men were at the mercy of the sea. Their small open craft was pushed far off course to the south and west. At last, the storm abated, and the men on board could relax. But where were they? Even their leader, an experienced sailor named Bjarni Herjolfsson, was not sure.

The sailors were Vikings, members of an adventurous tribe from northern Europe. They came from a region called *Scandinavia*, which includes present-day Norway, Sweden, and Denmark. The Vikings, also called Norsemen ("men from the North"), were fierce fighters who had terrorized Ireland, England, and Europe for more than 200 years. They were also brave seafarers who had developed sturdy longships, in which they explored the Atlantic.

For hundreds of years the Vikings told their children about the adventures of brave Norsemen like Bjarni Herjolfsson. Eventually, these tales were written down. Bjarni's was recorded in the *Greenlander's Saga* sometime during the 13th or 14th century.

During their expeditions from Scandinavia, the Norsemen had discovered many islands in the North Atlantic. They had settled on some of these, such as the Faeroe Islands (which are off the coast of Scotland), Iceland, and Greenland.

The *Saga* relates that Bjarni had been sailing for Greenland. This large island to the west of Iceland had been discovered four years earlier by a Norseman named Erik the Red. Bjarni's father, Herjolf, had been living in Iceland and decided to follow Erik to the new settlement in 985. Bjarni, who had been away when his father left, also decided to go to Greenland. He had never been there before, but he was confident that he could find the island, which was just a few days' sail away. Unfortunately, three days after he left Iceland, the storm hit and blew Bjarni and his men off course.

Once the storm ended, the ship was surrounded by fog. The sailors did not have compasses, maps, or other equipment that would help them **navigate** the mist-shrouded ocean. For the next several days, the ship wandered through the unknown waters.

After three days, the fog finally lifted. The next day, a sailor spotted land. However, Bjarni could see green hills and great forests. This did not fit with descriptions of Greenland. The interior of that island had tall mountains and **glaciers**—giant masses of ice. He turned his ship to the northeast.

Two days later, Bjarni and his men spotted land once again. This time, they saw a flat, wooded coast but no glaciers. Some of the men wanted to go ashore, but Bjarni refused to allow the ship to land. The Vikings continued sailing northeast. Three days later, they spotted another coast. This land looked too barren to be Greenland, however.

After four more days, the Vikings spotted yet another coast. "This is very like what I am told about Greenland, and here we will make for the land," Bjarni declared. The ship landed near a small settlement. As luck would have it, this was the very place that Herjolf was living. Father and son greeted each other joyfully.

Bjarni apparently never wanted to return and explore the lands that he had seen to the west. About 14 years after this voyage, Bjarni told some people about the coasts he had spotted. The Norsemen were amazed that he had not gone ashore. One of them decided he would explore to the west. His name was Leif, and he was the son of Erik the Red.

Leif bought a ship, gathered a crew of 36 men, and asked his father to come along and lead the expedition. Erik did not want to leave Greenland. He was growing older and was more interested in ruling his colony than in seeking new adventures. However, Erik reluctantly agreed to come along.

A crowd gathered around Brattahlid, Erik's farm on Greenland, as the Vikings prepared to leave. It was a warm spring day around the year 1000. Erik

This page from a 14th century Icelandic copy of the Greenlander's Saga *tells the story of Bjarni Herjolfsson and his off-course Viking voyage in* A.D. *986.*

the Red mounted his horse, leading a procession of Norsemen down the rocky path to the water's edge, where his son's longship was floating.

Suddenly, Erik's horse stumbled over a stone. The older man fell and injured himself. The meaning of this injury was clear: this journey would be unlucky for Erik the Red. He told his son, "It is not my destiny to discover more lands than this we are now living in," and turned back to Brattahlid.

It would be Leif Eriksson's destiny to become the most famous Viking explorer. Eriksson's amazing story, however, is merely one chapter in an epic of seafaring and exploration. The fearless Vikings would reach more new lands than any other European peoples of their time.

Danish raiders land in England in this illustration from a 12th-century book. The men at the right are walking down gangplanks to the shore. The book tells of a Viking raid on England that occurred in A.D. 886.

The Vikings 2

In the Old Norse language, the phrase *i viking* means to leave home and go raiding. To those who came into contact with the people of Scandinavia between the 8th and 14th centuries, the word "Viking" soon came to represent ferocious warriors. "From the fury of the Norsemen, good Lord deliver us," was a common prayer among those who lived along the coasts of northern Europe.

In the 700s, there were about two million people living in Scandinavia. However, throughout the next century, the population began to grow rapidly. Unfortunately, good farmland was limited in Scandinavia. Many Norsemen

Viking ships were typically carved with a dragon's head. This was to ward off evil spirits; it also struck fear into the hearts of enemies.

could not buy property because it was not available. They began eyeing the fertile lands to the south.

It was easy for the Vikings to sail to these lands. They were the best seamen of their time. They had developed two types of sturdy ships. One was a freight vessel called a **knörr** that could carry about 35 people. The other, and more famous, was the **drakkar** (dragon ship), a war vessel that was about 80 feet long. This type of Viking ship had a high **prow**, or front, that was carved to resemble a dragon. The superstitious Scandinavians believed this would protect the ship and its crew from evil spirits.

Both types of ships were made of oak boards that were overlapped. Animal fur or wool was stuffed into cracks to keep the ship from leaking. Each ship had a **keel**, a piece of wood that ran underneath the hull. This helped keep the ship stable in rough water and made it easier to steer. The ships were open to the elements, although a large piece of cloth could be pulled across the sides to protect passengers from wind and rain in the worst conditions.

The mast was nearly as high as the ship was long, and it was located in the center of the ship. This meant the dragon ship could be rigged to sail forward or backward. The single sail was made of wool. It was often dyed red to frighten those who saw the ship coming.

The Vikings did not depend on the wind alone for power. Each man had an oar. When there was no wind, or when there were tricky currents to negotiate, the sail was taken down and the men rowed together. One man would steer using a large rudder mounted to the side of the ship. When the men were rowing, they tied their shields to the sides of the ship for protection.

In addition to these large shields, which were often reinforced with iron, Viking warriors often wore an iron helmet and armor. This was usually a **breastplate**, a flat piece of iron padded with leather that was worn to protect the soldier's upper body. Wealthy Vikings might wear a **coat of mail**, which was made up of small iron rings sewn together on a leather shirt. These were more flexible and offered better protection in battle. Vikings carried either a double-bladed long sword or a heavy battle-ax, as well as a bow and arrows and a sharp knife.

Beginning around the end of the eighth century, people living in England, Ireland, and Europe greatly feared the approach of dragon ships. They had good reason to fear, for a visit from the Vikings often meant death and destruction.

In the 790s, Scandinavian colonies were established in northern Scotland. Vikings also settled on groups of islands—the Orkneys, Shetlands, and Hebrides—off the coast of England. The Vikings could attack from these bases.

The typical Viking raid (called a *strandhögg*) relied on surprise. With no warning, a group of drakkars would pull up onto a shore. A band of warriors would charge the town or settlement. If the defenders were beaten back, the Vikings would **pillage** homes and church buildings, robbing them of all valuable items. Then the buildings would be set on fire. The Vikings would return to their ships, taking their stolen treasure with them. Sometimes, captured defenders would be taken as well, to be sold as slaves.

These invasions were very effective. During the years 793 to 795, marauding Vikings attacked six monasteries in Ireland and England. Only one was able to successfully fight off the raiders. From 795 to 820, the Vikings raided Ireland 26 times.

In 830, Vikings from Norway conquered Armagh, an important city in the north of Ireland. In 839, a Viking leader named Thorgisl arrived in Ireland with a strong army. He conquered the Celtic tribes in the northern part of the island, and estab-

This is the top of a bishop's staff, called a crosier. The valuable relic was carved and bejeweled. Discovered in Viking ruins at Helgö, Sweden, it was probably taken during a raid on a monastery in Ireland.

lished a strong harbor city called Dyflinn (Dublin). For the next 160 years, groups of Vikings controlled Ireland. They founded other important cities, such as Limerick, Waterford, and Wexford.

By 851, Scandinavians were settling in England as well. These Vikings were attracted to the island's rich farmland and temperate climate. By the end of the ninth century, Vikings controlled the north and east of England. Because these invaders were from Denmark, this area became known as the Danelaw.

The Vikings did not limit their attacks to the islands of the North Atlantic. In the eighth century much of Europe had been united into a powerful empire by a French king, Charlemagne (Charles the Great). However, after his death in 814, the empire began to fall apart. A number of small countries were established. These became easy prey for Viking armies. They attacked cities on the coasts of Spain, France, and Italy. On Easter Sunday 843, an army of Vikings conquered the city of Paris.

Viking raiders often waited until religious holidays, such as Easter, to make their attacks. On these days, the Christian inhabitants of a targeted town would be participating in festivals and unprepared to fight.

Some kings tried to pay off the Vikings so that they would not attack their lands. When the Vikings returned to Paris in 885, the French king paid them 7,000 pounds of silver to leave peacefully. In 911, a French leader tried to bribe invading Vikings by offering their leader, Rolf, a large area of land where his men could live. In exchange, Rolf agreed to become a Christian and to protect France from other attacks. The land his men settled became known as Normandy—the land of the Norsemen.

Around the year 990, King Ethelred of England began to pay **tribute** to the Danish invaders who already controlled part of his island. This payment was called the *Danegeld* ("Dane's gold"). By 1013, the Vikings had taken 150,000 pounds of silver from the English. That year, a Danish king named Sven Forkbeard invaded England, intending to conquer the entire island. Although he was killed in the fighting, his son Knut the Great succeeded. Knut was crowned king of England in 1016. The Danes ruled the island until Knut's death in 1035.

While Danish and Norwegian Vikings were terrorizing Europe, others turned to the east. One of the first to make a voyage of exploration in this direction was named Ottar. A wealthy landowner

*This fierce-looking Viking helmet was found in Vals-
gärde, Sweden. There, and at Vendel, historians have
discovered burial sites dating from the seventh century.
Items found there provide insight into Scandinavian life.*

who lived on the west coast of Norway, Ottar was a
curious man. Around 880, he and a five-man crew
set sail along the coast of Norway to see how far it
extended to the north, and whether anyone lived

there. After three days, Ottar had gone as far as any man before him had ever ventured. He kept going for another three days and found that the coast turned to the east. Ottar had reached the North Cape, the very top of Norway.

The brave Scandinavian sailed east for four days, until the land veered to the south. After five more days of sailing, he came to the mouth of a river. Steering his ship up the river, he saw men hunting and fishing. He and his men killed 60 walruses in two days, then turned around and sailed for home.

Ottar's voyage was the first into the ocean above Norway (later named the Barents Sea) and the White Sea that borders the present-day country of Russia.

Other Vikings who sailed east around this time were less interested in exploration. These fierce fighters, many from Sweden, were looking for money and adventure. They began making raids into modern-

When King Alfred, a powerful Saxon king of England, heard about Ottar's discoveries, he asked Ottar to visit his court. There, the story of Ottar's voyage was written down and added to a large book on history and geography that Alfred's scribes were preparing.

day Finland and Russia. By some accounts, the Slavic people of Russia invited the Vikings. According to the *Russian Primary Chronicle*, a history written by monks in the 12th century, the Slavs told their neighbors, "Our country is rich and immense, but it is rent by disorder. Come and govern us and reign over us."

A Swedish Viking named Rurik did just that. He became governor of a small town and soon extended his control throughout the country. His successor, Oleg the Wise, built up the new Russian state. His capital, the city of Kiev, soon became an important center of trade and culture.

> **The Slavic people of Finland called one tribe of Vikings *Rus*. This may be where Russia got its name.**

The Vikings also traveled across Russia on the Volga, Dnieper, and Vistula rivers. From these waterways, they could reach the Black and Caspian Seas and attack settlements in eastern Europe. In 907 a huge Viking army reached the important and wealthy city of Constantinople. The Vikings were paid tribute so that they would not attack the city. In 941 other Viking raiders attempted to sack the city, which they called Miklagard ("big city"), but it was strongly defended and these attacks failed.

Vikings even made it to Greece and the Middle East. On the Greek island of Delos, Viking runes have been found carved on a stone lion. And in 1040, Ingvar the Great Voyager led 30 ships in an invasion of Middle Eastern lands held by the Muslims. The attack failed when Ingvar was killed the next year somewhere in Syria.

By this time, the Viking period had reached its highest point. The children of Scandinavians who had invaded Europe and Asia decades earlier were becoming assimilated into the local cultures. One of the last great Viking heroes was Harald the Ruthless, the king of Norway. In 1066, he decided to invade England, planning to reclaim the island kingdom of Knut the Great. However, the Saxon king, Harold, led a successful defense. At the battle of Stamford Bridge, Harald the Ruthless was killed.

However, two days after Harald's defeat, Duke William of Normandy led a Norman army across the English Channel. At the Battle of Hastings, King Harold was defeated and killed. William, now called the Conqueror, was crowned king of England. The arrival of the Normans, who themselves were descended from Vikings, ended Saxon rule of the island.

Norse sailors land on the coast of Iceland in this colorful illustration. One of the main reasons the Vikings attacked and explored was to gain land of their own, because Scandinavia was very crowded.

Into the Atlantic

3

nformation about the Vikings' activities comes from three main sources. One of these is historical accounts made by the Vikings' victims after they were attacked. English, Irish, and European monasteries kept daily records, for example. More information comes from the sagas. These are stories of Viking achievements that were told to generation after generation, until they were finally written down around the 13th century. Two important collections of these stories are the *Landnamabók* and the *Flateyjarbók*, which contain both the *Greenlander's Saga* and the *Saga of Erik the Red*. A third source of information is archaeological evidence, such as the remains of settlements. This is often used to confirm or disprove the information provided in contemporary accounts or the sagas.

From these sources, modern-day historians know that the Vikings did not just invade the known world. In their desire for plunder and new settlements, they also set off in search of new lands.

The Vikings were not the first to sail deep into the unknown waters of the Atlantic, however. The Irish had already been sailing these waters for hundreds of years. The people of Ireland were **pagans**, until they were converted to Christianity in the fifth century by Saint Patrick. The Irish became dedicated Christians. They established **monasteries** (places dedicated to religious study and learning) throughout the country. Some religious men became **missionaries**. They traveled far and wide to convert others to the faith. They preached both throughout Ireland and in neighboring lands. Irish

Eventually, the Irish found their way to Greenland, and some historians believe that Irish monks landed in the New World before the Vikings. However, there are not enough facts to prove this theory.

monks spread Christianity to England, Wales, France, and Germany. In frail boats called **coracles**, they also sailed west to find unknown lands.

In the sixth century, Saint Brendan, an Irish priest, discovered groups of islands in the North Atlantic. These were the Faeroe Islands and the Shetland Islands. By A.D. 700, an Irish settlement was established on the Faeroe Islands. (It was abandoned by the time Viking settlers arrived about 100 years later.) In 770, Irish monks landed on Iceland, which they called Thule. It was shortly after this time that the Vikings' raids on Europe began.

According to the *Landnamabók*, the Scandinavian discovery of Iceland occurred sometime in the ninth century. One story tells of a Swedish sailor named Gardar who was traveling to collect money owed to his wife. "When he sailed through the Pentland Firth he got into bad weather and his ship was driven out into the western sea," records the *Landnamabók*. "He struck land east of Horn, where there was a harbor. Gardar sailed around the country and determined that it was an island."

Gardar landed on the island and spent the winter there. When he returned, he called the place Gardarsholm (Gardar's Island).

Another story tells of a Norwegian named Naddodd who also landed on the island around this time. "[Naddodd and his men] climbed the highest mountains to see if they could discern any dwellings of people or smokes, but they saw none," says the *Landnamabók*. "As they were sailing away from the country, a heavy snow fell on the land; therefore they named it Snowland."

In 865, a Danish chief named Floki Vilgerdarson sailed west from the Faeroe Islands. According to the legends, he brought three birds with him in a cage. After he sailed into unknown waters, Floki set the first bird free, hoping it would fly toward land. The first bird flew back the way the Vikings had come. A few days later, he set the second bird free. This one flew up and then landed in the ship's rigging. Floki knew his ship must be far from land. When he let the final bird loose some time later, it flew ahead. The Viking sailors followed this bird until they saw an island rising from the frigid ocean.

Floki and his men sailed around the island until they found a good place to land. They called this spot Vatnsfjord. Because they found the waters were full of fish, they built homes to spend the winter. In the spring, Floki climbed a large mountain to survey

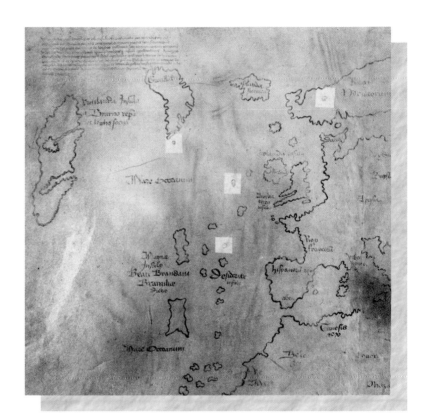

Islands in the North Atlantic are clearly marked on the "Vinland Map," a Viking relic on display at Yale University. The map shows lands discovered by the Vikings. The three islands across the top of the map are Iceland, (right), Greenland (center), and the area explored by Leif Eriksson (left). The inscriptions are in Latin.

the countryside. He could see large icebergs in the waters around the island, so he called it Iceland.

Floki and his men stayed in Iceland for another winter, then returned home. Although Floki had been unhappy with Iceland's harsh climate, other members of his crew were more enthusiastic. They told many others about the island.

Around 870, two foster brothers named Ingólfur Arnason and Leif Hrodmarsson were forced to give up their land in Norway. They decided to leave the country and see the island that Floki and his men had discovered years earlier. They sailed a knörr west until they reached Iceland. After spending the winter there, they returned to Norway. Ingólfur and Leif planned to bring others with them and establish a colony.

Ingólfur stayed in Norway to raise interest in the colony, while Leif went on a Viking raid to Ireland seeking money and slaves. It was not until 874 that the two men were able to return. This time, each took a ship containing family members and friends, supplies and farm animals, and slaves that Leif had captured in Ireland.

The two men landed and established their settlements approximately 60 miles apart. In the spring, Leif's slaves revolted and killed him and his men, then kidnapped the women and fled to a small island nearby. When Ingólfur learned about this uprising, he and his men hunted down and killed the slaves, rescuing the women.

A Viking rune stone. The Norsemen often carved inscriptions into rocks or landmarks when they reached new lands, such as Iceland.

Ingólfur and his family settled near the Olfusa River. He called his settlement Reykjavíc, which means "smoky bay," because of steam from nearby hot springs. (Today, Reykjavíc is the oldest city in Iceland, and Ingólfur Arnason and Leif Hrodmarsson are considered the country's founders.)

Within a few years, large numbers of Scandinavians began to settle in Iceland. These first colonists found Irish monks living there. But as the newcomers established their own settlements, they killed off or chased away the Irish.

A Viking burial ground in Iceland. The small island quickly became populated, as Scandinavians traveled there to settle and farm.

The first Viking settlers found that the interior of the island was not a very good place to live. In some areas, hot steam from active volcanoes poured out of cracks in the ground. Other areas were covered by glaciers. However, along the coasts of the island were plains and valleys where the Vikings could farm and raise cattle. There were other things that made Iceland an attractive place to settle. There were plenty of fish in the waters around the island. There were large forests of birch trees, and rich deposits of iron that could be used by blacksmiths to make tools and weapons.

Between 870 and 930, more than 10,000 Viking colonists landed in Iceland. The island's population soon grew to more than 50,000 people. Within a few years the people living in Iceland were faced with the same problems they had hoped to leave behind in Scandinavia. There was no room for more people to settle, and the island did not have the food or resources to support its population.

This overcrowding made some of the Icelanders restless. They began to wonder if there might be more attractive lands to the west.

Erik the Red's Discovery

Despite its name, Greenland is a country of ice and snow, with large mountains and huge glaciers. The climate was not as harsh when Erik the Red settled there, however; from the 9th to the 13th centuries temperatures were warmer than they are today.

4

Around 960, a man named Thorvald Asvaldsson was living in Norway. When a man in his town insulted him, Thorvald became angry. He killed the man in a fight. As punishment, he was ordered to leave Norway for three years. This was a common punishment, called **exile**. Thorvald went to Iceland, taking his family with him. One of his sons, a redhead named Erik, was probably about five years old when the family left Norway.

When Thorvald arrived in Iceland, most of the good land had already been taken. He claimed a rocky farm in the northwest part of the island. There, his son grew up. Erik the Red, as friends nicknamed him, shared his father's temper. When he was about 20 years old, Erik became involved in a feud with another family and killed several men. His punishment was the same as his father's had been: a three-year exile from Iceland.

Erik could have returned to Norway, or he could have sailed to other Viking outposts on Atlantic islands such as the Faeroes. However, he decided instead to sail west in search of an island that, so the stories told, had been spotted in that direction. He had heard old men talk about a sailor named Gunnbjörn, who had claimed to see a snow-capped mountain to the west of Iceland. The date of this sighting is uncertain, but it probably was between 877 and 900. Over the winter of 981 Erik outfitted a ship and prepared to explore.

In the spring of 982, Erik left Iceland, probably in a longship. He brought his family, his slaves, and two other families that wanted to go along—probably 30 to 40 people in all. The boat also carried farm animals and hay to feed them on the journey.

There was little shelter in Viking longships making the journey across the ocean. Erik the Red's ship probably looked a lot like the one illustrated here.

The sagas do not give many details about Erik's voyage. He had to sail due west about 450 miles to reach the coast of Greenland. Even after he spotted land, Erik could not beach his ship immediately. Fog and drifting chunks of ice forced him to turn south and follow the coastline. He rounded Cape Farewell, the southernmost point of Greenland, and began sailing north along the western shore. This side of the island was protected from Atlantic storms, and there was less ice. While Erik and his men saw a glacier covering the center of the island, there were broad plains of grass between the shore and the ice. There were sheltered places where a ship could be safely anchored. Berries grew on the shore and the waters were filled with fish.

For the next three years, Erik and his men explored the island. They named the place where they landed Eriksfjord (Erik's fjord) and built homes and barns there. They also looked for places where settlements could be established. By the time Erik's exile ended, he was determined to return to Iceland and bring back colonists. With that in mind, he named the island Greenland. "He argued that men would be all the more drawn to go there if it had an attractive name," reports the *Saga of Erik the Red*.

Erik was welcomed back to Iceland, and many people were interested in hearing about his discovery. Overcrowding had caused many problems in Iceland, including years of *famine*. The news that an uninhabit-

---

Although Erik the Red may have seen the island as a "green land," today we know this name is inaccurate. Greenland lies within the Arctic Circle. Only about 18 percent of its 1.3-million-square-mile land area is free of ice.

ed land lay just a few weeks' sail away was very exciting. Many people were willing to make the dangerous ocean crossing for a chance to claim large estates in Greenland.

In the summer of 985, Erik the Red set out for Greenland again. This time, he led 25 ships west, bearing colonists and the items they would need to survive. On board Erik's ship were his wife, Thjodhild, and their sons, Thorvald, Thorstein, and Leif.

Not all of the ships reached Greenland. Some of them were lost in a storm. Others turned back to Iceland. However, 14 ships landed, bringing between 400 and 500 settlers. They spread out along about 120 miles of coastline. Each family claimed land and established a farm.

The area where most of the colonists lived was called the Eastern Settlement. (Today, this is the port of Julianehåb.) Erik the Red was recognized as their leader. He built a large house, which he called Brattahlid, at Eriksfjord. A smaller group of colonists founded the Western Settlement farther north along the coast. This settlement grew up around the Godthåb Fjord.

The year after Erik and his followers returned, the *Greenlander's Saga* indicates that Bjarni Herjolfsson sailed from Iceland to find his father in Green land. During that fateful trip, he spotted lands to the west before he reached his father's house.

The Greenland colony prospered. Each summer, new Norsemen came to settle in Greenland. At first, the colonists farmed and raised sheep and cattle. They also came to depend on hunting and fishing for food. Settlers discovered that they could hunt seals from ice. Whales, walruses, and polar bears were also popular game. There were also plenty of eider ducks, an arctic sea bird.

Ships came regularly from Norway, bringing supplies that the colony needed. Among the most important items brought to the colony was timber. Greenland did not have large trees that could be cut down and used to build houses and ships. Instead, the island's trees were small and useful for nothing but firewood. The Greenlanders depended on the regular shipments of timber from Norway.

In exchange for the supplies, the Greenlanders traded the valuable furs they collected. The colonists also traded strips of tough leather, which were made from walrus or whale skins, and eider duck feathers that could be used to make warm blankets and coats.

Around the year 1000, Erik the Red's son Leif decided to go exploring to the west. The *Greenlander's Saga* relates that Leif was in Greenland when he heard Bjarni Herjolfsson's story. He then visited Bjarni's farm, bought his knörr, and prepared to seek the new lands.

The *Saga of Erik the Red* tells a different story. It does not mention Bjarni Herjolfsson or his earlier voyage at all. Instead, this saga says that Leif was returning home from a visit to the court of the king of Norway, Olaf Tryggvason, when his ship was blown off course. According to this story Leif was the first to spot the unknown lands to the west of Greenland.

> Even among the Vikings, Leif Eriksson was considered an expert sailor. He had been the first man to sail directly from Greenland to Scotland without making the usual stop at Iceland. This, and his other sailing adventures, had earned him the nickname "Leif the Lucky."

It does not matter whether Leif Eriksson and his men intended to search for new lands or arrived there by accident. They would become the first Europeans to set foot in North America.

Vinland

Are these Viking buildings in Newfoundland all that is left of Leifsbudir, *the dwellings built by Leif Eriksson and his men about 1,000 years ago in North America? Many historians believe they may be, although the exact location where Eriksson landed has never been determined.*

5

eif and his men followed the coast of Greenland north for several hundred miles past the Western Settlement. Then they turned west, tracing Bjarni's route in reverse. When Leif sighted land, he ordered the ship to be anchored. The men went ashore and found the land was rugged and barren. Leif named this place Helluland, which means "flatstone land." Today, historians believe this was Baffin Island, a large island to the north of Canada.

A statue of the most famous Viking explorer, Leif Eriksson. According to the Greenlander's Saga, Leif was "big and strong, of striking appearance, shrewd, and, in every respect, a temperate and fair-dealing man."

Setting out again, Leif spotted a flat, wooded coast. When his men landed, they found long white beaches leading up to forests of valuable trees. Leif named this place Markland ("wood land"). Today, no one is certain where Markland was. It may have been Labrador, on the east coast of Canada, or Nova Scotia.

Returning to their knörr, Leif and his men continued sailing southwest. When they reached the green, fertile land that Bjarni had reported, they sailed up a river and landed on the banks of a lake. The men built huts for temporary shelter and went inland to explore. They found large salmon in the rivers and an abundance of timber. The climate of this new land was much milder than that of Greenland and Iceland.

Leif and his men decided to stay for the winter, and they built a large house. Once the house was built, Leif divided his men into two groups. One would stay behind and protect the house; the other would explore the land.

One night, when both groups were together at Leifsbudir ("Leif's house," as the campsite was called), they realized a man was missing. His name was Tyrkir, and he was a relative of Leif's. Before they could start a search, however, Tyrkir arrived. He excitedly told his comrades that he had found grapevines–a rare discovery.

Leif and his men cut down some of the vines and stored them in their ship. They also collected berries and wild wheat, as well as long wooden beams. In the spring, Leif led his crew back to Greenland. He named the land where he had stayed Vinland ("wine land") because of the grapes that grew there.

For many years, the exact location of Vinland was disputed. Most people believed that Leif had landed somewhere on the Atlantic coast of North

America between Newfoundland and Long Island. Others argued that because grapes do not grow that far north, Vinland was farther to the south—possibly even in Georgia. In 1960, however, Norwegian archaeologists Helge Ingstad and Anne Stine Ingstad found Norse ruins at L'Anse aux Meadows on the northern tip of Newfoundland. The ruins indicated that Vikings had lived there around the year 1000.

After Leif returned from Vinland, there is no evidence that he ever returned. (He may have gone back during brief visits to gather timber from Vinland or Markland, however.) It would be up to Erik's other sons, Thorvald and Thorstein, to continue the exploration of Vinland.

A year or two after Leif's return, Thorvald borrowed his brother's knörr and sailed west with about 30 men. They spent the winter in the houses that Leif and his men had built at Leifsbudir. In the spring, they went exploring in Vinland and Markland. While walking on a sandy headland, Thorvald told the others, "This is a lovely place, and I should like to make my home here."

Just then the men spotted three mounds on the shore. When they got closer, they discovered the mounds were boats made of skin stretched over a

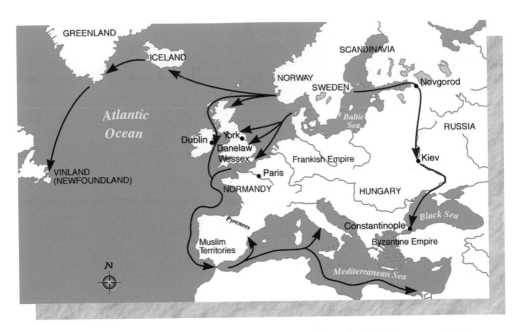

This map shows the routes of many Viking expeditions. The Vikings had already fought their way through most of the known world before setting out through the Atlantic to western lands, such as Vinland.

wooden frame, like the Irish coracles. Underneath each boat were three Native Americans. The Vikings attacked and killed eight of the men, but not before Thorvald Eriksson was shot with an arrow. Some of the Vikings chased the surviving Indian, who escaped into a ravine, while the others carried their wounded leader back to their camp. "We have certainly discovered a good country, but we do not seem likely to have long use of it," Thorvald predicted. Before dying from his wound, Thorvald

Although Vinland seemed to be a good place to live, only a few Vikings attempted to sail to the faraway new land and create a settlement there. The most ambitious attempt was led by Thorfinn Karlsefni around 1006.

asked his men to bury him at the headland and to call the place Krossanes ("Cross Cape").

According to the *Saga of Erik the Red*, Thorstein Eriksson then led an expedition to Vinland. However, this voyage did not go smoothly. "They encountered difficulties at sea," the saga relates. "Their ship kept being driven back and forth across the sea. Toward autumn they returned to Greenland, discouraged and tired. Winter was already beginning when they reached Eriksfjord." Thorstein died over the winter, leaving a widow named Gudrid.

In the summer of 1005, a wealthy merchant from Iceland named Thorfinn Karlsefni visited Eriksfjord. He fell in love with Gudrid and asked Erik the Red for permission to marry her. Erik agreed, and they were married at Brattahlid over the winter. In the spring of 1006, Gudrid and Karlsefni led a new group of explorers—65 men, 5 women, and some livestock—to Vinland. This time, the Vikings were trying to colonize the new land.

When Karlsefni and Gudrid arrived at Leifsbudir, they found a dying whale that had been washed up on the beach. They killed the monstrous sea mammal, and it kept them well supplied with food. The fishing and hunting were also good. They spent the winter at Leifsbudir.

The next spring, Karlsefni and his men continued their explorations. The *Saga of Erik the Red* says that they sailed up a river and found a land they called Hop. (This Icelandic word is pronounced like the English word "hope" and means a small bay.) "In this country they discovered fields of self-sown wheat wherever the land was low, but [grapevines] wherever there were hills," the saga related. "Their brook was full of fish. . . . There were great numbers of wild animals of every kind in the forest."

While Karlsefni's men were camped at Hop, they had their first encounter with Native Americans. A group of them rowed up in their skin boats to take a look at the newcomers, then rowed away. The Scandinavians called the natives *Skraelings,* which means "ugly men." These Native Americans may have been members of the Algonquin tribe.

When Karlsefni returned to the settlement, he built a wooden fence around it for protection from the Skraelings. Over the winter of 1007–8, his wife gave birth to their son, whom they named Snorri. He was the first European born in America.

When spring arrived, the Viking colonists had further trouble with the Skraelings. During one visit, the Native Americans tried to steal some weapons, and fighting broke out. More serious battles followed. Even though the land was fertile, Karlsefni knew that the natives would continue attacking the outnumbered colonists. He decided to return home.

The final effort to colonize Vinland that was recorded in the sagas involved a daughter of Erik the Red named Freydis. According to the *Greenlander's Saga*, after Thorfinn Karlsefni's return, Freydis and her husband, Thorvard, led a group of 60 colonists from Greenland to the new land. At the same time, two brothers named Helgi and Finnbogi led a similarly sized group of Norwegians to Vinland. The two groups had planned to explore and colonize together. However, Freydis started an argument between the two crews, and the Greenlanders killed the Norwegians. The survivors then returned to Greenland.

After this, attempts to colonize Vinland apparently ended. The resources of the Greenland colony were already being stretched to the limit. For decades after Leif Eriksson's voyage, the Vikings may have returned to Markland for timber. However, their exploration of North America was finished.

> The *Saga of Erik the Red* tells a different story about Freydis. This saga relates that she was a member of Thorfinn Karlsefni's expedition. In a battle against the Skraelings, she single-handedly scared away the attacking Indians with a sword.

A replica of a Viking longship sails through a fjord in Greenland in 1997. The men on board were attempting to re-create Leif Eriksson's 1,900-mile journey to North America.

The Fate of the Greenland Colony

6

At its height, the Greenland colony had some 4,000 inhabitants. Around the time of Leif Eriksson's voyage to Vinland, the island was converted to Christianity, and a number of churches were built in the Eastern Settlement.

As the years went on, the people of Greenland grew more and more dependent on trade ships from Iceland and Norway. The soil was too poor to grow grain, so farmers raised sheep and cattle. Grain for baking was highly valued. Also, although Greenland had large deposits of iron ore, it had little coal or timber that could be used as fuel in furnaces to melt the iron. Therefore, iron tools and weapons had to be brought from outside. Long timbers to build houses and ships, glassware, linens, and other items were also imported to the island colony.

In the 13th century, the Greenland colony began to decline. There were several reasons for this. One is that the weather, already harsh, became even worse around the year 1200. The world entered a period of global cooling that has been called the Little Ice Age. The winters in Greenland grew longer and colder. It was already difficult to raise food in the colony; this just made things harder on the Greenlanders.

As the weather grew colder, Indians began to migrate from the northern part of Greenland to the southern areas where the Vikings had established their colonies. While these Indians were also called Skraelings by the Vikings, they were also known as Thule. (In fact, they were Inuit, or Eskimos.) In some cases there were friendly relations between the Indians and colonists, but in others there was fighting between the two groups.

Another reason for the colony's failure was a loss of trade. Iceland became an official part of the country of Norway in 1261. Greenland gave up its independence the next year when the Norwegian government promised that more supply ships would be sent to the colony.

Unfortunately, Norway was not very concerned with its tiny frontier outpost in Greenland, and the number of supply ships dwindled. Because the items that the Greenlanders produced could be purchased more cheaply in Norway, there was no incentive for the ships to visit the colony. At one time several ships had visited Greenland each year, but soon supply ships were arriving only once every two years.

Worse, the government of Norway ordered the Icelanders not to trade with Greenland. The government had given a **monopoly** on trade with Greenland to the Norwegian port of Bergen. This meant only ships from Bergen could trade with the colony. Others who did were breaking the law and could be punished.

By 1342, the Western Settlement had been abandoned. The flow of settlers had long since dried up. The people of the colony may have died off, left to live with the Thule, or moved south to join the Eastern Settlement.

*The remains of a Viking settlement in Greenland. The
voyages and adventures of the Vikings have fascinated
many people through the years.*

When ships did arrive at the Eastern Settlement
in the second half of the 14th century, some
colonists left with them for Iceland or Norway. The
last regular supply ship from Norway landed around
1367. In 1406, a group of Icelanders sailed to Greenland. They stayed there for four years. When they
left in 1410, they took the last news of the colony
with them.

In 1540, a sailor from Iceland was blown off course while trying to reach Germany. He and his men landed in Greenland and went ashore at the Eastern Settlement. There, they found empty houses and barns. They saw one dead man and took his knife as a souvenir. In the 1580s, the English mariner John Davis sailed around Greenland, but he saw no signs of life.

The end of the Greenland colony marked the end of the Viking age. New powers had risen in Europe: England, France, Spain, and Portugal. The lands that the Vikings had discovered to the west were remembered only in obscure legends. It would not be until the voyages of Christopher Columbus, nearly 500 years after Leif Eriksson, that interest in the New World would be rekindled.

Chronology

793   Vikings attack the monastery of St. Cuthbert on the island of Lindisfarne, off the coast of England; this is the first in a series of Viking raids on England and Ireland.

835   The Danelaw is created in England.

843   The Vikings sack Paris.

865   Floki Vilgerdarson lands in Iceland.

874   Ingólfur Arnason and Leif Hrodmarsson establish the first permanent settlements in Iceland.

880   Ottar, a Norwegian landowner, explores the Arctic Ocean to the east above Scandinavia.

911   The Viking leader Rolf is given land in France and establishes the duchy of Normandy.

982   Erik the Red goes into exile from Iceland; over the next three years he discovers and explores Greenland.

985   Erik the Red leads 25 ships west from Iceland to Greenland to establish a permanent settlement; 14 ships, containing 400 to 500 colonists, reach the island.

986   Bjarni Herjolfsson's ship is blown off course; he and his men spot land to the west of Greenland, but do not explore.

1000   Leif Eriksson sails west with a crew of 36 men and discovers Helluland, Markland, and Vinland.

1003   Thorvald Eriksson is killed by a Native American's arrow in the New World.

1006   Thorfinn Karlsefni and his wife Gudrid lead 65 men and 5 women to Vinland to establish a colony.

1007 Karlsefni and his men discover Hop, a landlocked bay, where they encounter Native Americans for the first time; during the winter Gudrid gives birth to a son, Snorri, who is the first European child born in North America.

1008 Karlsefni leads his party back to Greenland.

1066 The Normans, under Duke William, conquer England.

1261 Iceland becomes part of the state of Norway.

1262 Greenland joins the state of Norway.

1342 The Western Settlement is abandoned.

1367 The last regular supply ship from Norway is sent to Greenland.

1410 The last news from the Greenland colony is sent to Iceland.

1540 Sailors blown off course land in Greenland and find the Eastern Settlement deserted.

1960 Norwegian archaeologists Helge Ingstad and Anne Stine Ingstad discover Norse ruins at L'Anse aux Meadows on the northern tip of Newfoundland. They believe these are the remains of a Viking camp in Vinland.

Glossary

breastplate—armor, usually a flat metal plate padded with leather, that is worn to protect the chest.

coat of mail—a shirt made of metal rings or mesh, worn for protection in battle.

coracle—a small boat made of animal skin stretched over a wooden frame.

drakkar—a Viking warship, also called a dragon ship.

exile—to banish or expel a person from his or her home country.

famine—a great shortage of food.

glacier—a large body of ice that covers a land surface.

keel—the main piece of timber in the bottom center of a boat, used to help keep the craft steady in rough waters.

knörr—a Viking freight vessel, usually about 54 feet long.

missionary—a person who travels to spread his or her religion to people in other lands.

monastery—a place where people who have taken religious vows live. In the Middle Ages, monasteries were the centers of learning in Europe.

monopoly—exclusive control of a supply or product.

navigate—to steer a course through water.

pagan—a person who follows a religion in which multiple gods are worshipped.

pillage—the act of seizing and taking away valuable items during war.

prow–the high projecting front of a ship.

Scandinavia–a region of northern Europe that includes the present-day countries of Norway, Sweden, and Denmark.

tribute–a payment from one country to another to acknowledge submission or as the price of protection.

Further Reading

Cohat, Yves. *The Vikings: Lords of the Sea.* New York: Harry N. Abrams, 1992.

Jones, Gwyn. *A History of the Vikings.* New York: Oxford University Press, 1984.

Lewis, Richard S. *From Vinland to Mars.* New York: Quadrangle Books, 1976.

Page, R. I. *Chronicles of the Vikings: Records, Memorials, and Myths.* Toronto: University of Toronto Press, 1996.

Stefansson, Vilhjalmur. *Great Adventures and Explorations: From the Earliest Times to the Present, as Told by the Explorers Themselves.* New York: The Dial Press, 1947.

Stefoff, Rebecca. *The Viking Explorers.* New York: Chelsea House, 1993.

Streissguth, Thomas. *Life Among the Vikings.* San Diego: Lucent Books, 1999.

Picture Credits

JIM GALLAGHER is the author of more than a dozen books for young adults, including biographies of Vasco da Gama, Sir Francis Drake, Ferdinand Magellan, and Hernando de Soto in the Chelsea House series EXPLORERS OF NEW WORLDS. A former newspaper editor and publisher, he lives near Philadelphia.